MOODS OF
MID WALES

NICK JENKINS

HALSGROVE

First published in Great Britain in 2005

Title page photograph: **Red kite**

British Library Cataloguing-in-Publication Data
A CIP record for this title is available from the British Library

ISBN 1 84114 295 6

HALSGROVE
Halsgrove House
Lower Moor Way
Tiverton, Devon EX16 6SS
Tel: 01884 243242
Fax: 01884 243325
email: sales@halsgrove.com
website: www.halsgrove.com

Printed and bound by D'Auria Industrie Grafiche Spa, Italy

INTRODUCTION

In my formative years I watched with more than just a passing interest as my father took photographs everywhere we went. His slide shows became family events. Subconsciously I guess, this was what started to kindle my interest in photography and when my brother-in-law and I walked a number of the National Parks together, this finally shaped the direction that my images would take.

Many years were spent photographing wild and remote places, but my pictures somehow just failed to really convey the sense of ruggedness or grandeur that I experienced when 'out there'. All the mountains or people seemed so far off into the picture as to be barely discernable!

Finally I made it my business to address this shortcoming and, on joining a local camera club (Gwynfa, Llantrisant, for those who know me), I slowly started to understand where I was going wrong. My awareness of how to actually compose an image, as against simply snapping a nice scene, started to grow and before long, my pictures slowly started to make more sense. Walking became a lesser priority and capturing the beauty of this country started to take precedence. I still walked (and still walk) but the emphasis has definitely shifted in favour of photography.

I cut my photographic teeth in the Brecon Beacons but soon started to yearn for somewhere else to explore. The logical step for me as to drift further north, over the Eppynt Mountains (Mynydd Eppynt) and into an area so vast that it initially just confused me. This was the Heart of Wales, roughly covering the county of Powys, previously made up of Breconshire (the northern bit), Radnorshire, Montgomeryshire and a chunk of Ceredigion (or Cardiganshire as it was also known).

If I am to be honest, Mid Wales is still an enigma to me. I am drawn to the isolated hamlets and villages. I am fascinated by the remoteness of some of the hill farms, so far off the beaten track. Much use is made of local timber in the building of farms and barns, as well as the beautiful country churches.

I love the vast, high tracts of emptiness, with nothing but remote moorland and mile after mile of forest. I love the bubbling streams and rushing rivers as they cut their way through the Cambrian slate rocks. I find irresistible the mild eccentricity that still sees the world bog-snorkelling championships held annually near Abergwesyn.

But, most of all, I just love that feeling of 'being away from it all' which rural Mid Wales so powerfully conveys. Put all this together and the landscape lover and photographer is just spoiled for choice. Maybe the reason for my fascination with the wild fastnesses of Mid Wales will become clear to me one day – a process I am in no hurry to complete!

The images I have selected for this book are my attempt to seek to convey to you my feeling for that remoteness. It is by no means intended as a complete or comprehensive portfolio of Mid Wales – to attempt such an undertaking would take years. But if it tempts you to explore this truly wonderful area for yourself then I will have more than fulfilled my mission.

Nick Jenkins
July 2005

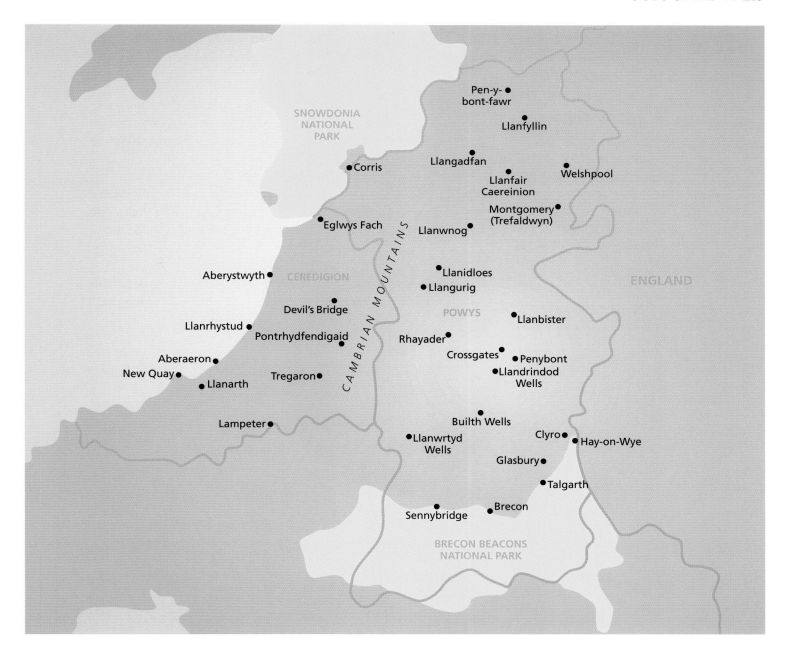

DEDICATION

This book is dedicated to Steve Day, a wonderful photographer, a true inspiration and real friend, who sadly died of a brain tumour in 2004, but who fought it to the very end.

Trees above the confluence of Afon Doethie and Afon Tywi
These gnarled old trees seemed to be trying to tell me something as they waved about in the breeze.

The summit of Dinas Rock above Afon Tywi
*This is where the legendary outlaw Twm Sion
Catti supposedly had his cave – a truly remote
spot even now. It must have seemed like
the middle of nowhere in his day, with
no lanes to guide the traveller.*

Opposite: **Cwm Graig-ddu on the
northern edge of Mynydd Eppynt**
*A deep and steep-sided gorge, frequented
only by sheep and peregrine falcons.
Mist frequently fills this valley
early in the morning.*

**Afon Irfon below the Devil's Staircase,
Abergwesyn Common**
*The river split by a large boulder was just crying
out to be photographed. I was happy to oblige.*

Abergwesyn Common
Managed by the National Trust, this area is remote and rugged – perfect for unhurried landscape photography.

Fish pond at Abbey Cwmhir, alongside the Clywedog Brook
There is very little left of the abbey, but it is perhaps best known as the last resting place of Llewelyn ap Gruffydd (Llewellyn the Last), whose modern memorial lies at the west end of the abbey ruins.

Abbey Cwmhir village
Wherever you go in Mid Wales, sheep are never far away. These two watched my every move as I photographed them.

Opposite: **Abbey Cwmhir village**
Abbey Cwmhir is a village almost locked into a time warp. Only the odd passing car breaks the age-old silence.

Barn near Llaithddu
The remoteness of this barn appealed to me as being typical of rural Mid Wales. Nearby, curlews were calling with their haunting burble across the large, empty wilderness.

Church of St Cewydd, Disserth
This wonderful church is closely associated with Francis Kilvert, the Victorian diarist/curate. It escaped the ravages of Victorian 'restoration' so the interior is a wonderful time capsule filled with seventeenth-century carved pews.

Shop front at Beguildy, between Newtown and Knighton
An intriguing collection of old advertising boards bedeck the front of the village store.

The graveyard at Soar y Mynydd Chapel near Llyn Brianne
*The gravestones at this remote chapel are inscribed in Welsh. The setting sun
just glanced across the front of the stones as I arrived.*

Penygarreg Dam, Elan Valley
*Taken just before the heavens emptied and lightning
ripped across the sky. This shot was exposed
for around one second to try to capture the
water as it cascaded over the dam.*

**Stream flowing into
Garreg Ddu Reservoir, Elan Valley**
*This is just one of many little streams
constantly topping up the Elan Reservoirs.
It just appeared out of nowhere
through a dense woodland.*

Craig Coch Dam, Elan Valley
The Victorians really took trouble over the architecture of these Welsh dams. It was completed in 1904 and opened by King Edward VII. The water was earmarked for the citizens and industry of far-off Birmingham.

Bridge over the Afon Elan, Elan Valley
Between the turbulence of the water cascading over the dams, all is peace and tranquillity.

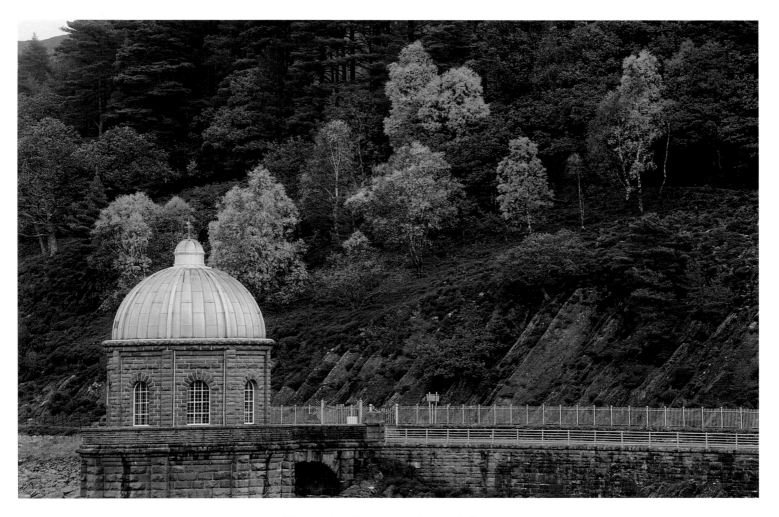

Foel Extraction Tower on Garreg Ddu Dam
The contrast of nature and man's intervention always intrigues me.

Opposite: **The Afon Elan
at Elan Village**
*The River Elan as it passes through the
austere stone village, built to house the
workers on this huge reservoir project.*

Nant Gwyllt Stream, Elan Valley
*Percy Shelley once lived where
this stream empties into Caban Coch
Reservoir. I love photographing
waterfalls, and this is one
of my favourites.*

Pen y garreg Reservoir, Elan Valley
*The inky blackness of the water on a grey autumn day really stood out amid
the greens and browns of the surrounding hills.*

Opposite: **Afon Tywi near Dinas Rock**
This wild Welsh river, tamed by the mighty Llyn Brianne Dam just upstream, still retains much of its natural beauty.

Church of St Cewydd, Aberedw
St Cewydd is the Welsh patron saint of rain – which must make him a pretty busy saint then!
Francis Kilvert once declared Aberedw to be one of his very favourite places.

Tynllidiart Farm, Elan Valley
This typical hill farm sums up the sense of isolation of farming in Mid Wales.

Cwm Graig Ddu, Mynydd Eppynt
*A mist-free view of this steep-sided valley,
looking across to the Irfon Valley.*

Falls on the Afon Tywi
White water crashing over rocks on a bright summer day – my idea of bliss.

Y Bwa Arch
*An arch of some stature on the road between Devil's Bridge and Cwm Ystwyth. It was built in 1812
by Thomas Johnes to commemorate the Golden Jubilee of George III two years before.*

Soar y Mynydd Chapel near Llyn Brianne
This remote chapel is lost in a valley just north of the enormous reservoir of Llyn Brianne.
From here green lanes lead into the hills behind.

Craig Clungwyn in the Doethie Valley
Such is the isolation of this area, you can walk these hills all day and not see another soul.

Memorial to Llewelyn the Last at Cilmeri
*This stone is said to mark the spot where Llewelyn was killed in 1282 as he sought
to rally support against Edward I in the southern part of Wales.*

Pines on Caban Coch Reservoir, Elan Valley

Forestry is a major source of income here, and it somehow doesn't appear too intrusive in this land of water and trees.

Sheep at Abergwesyn
No matter how far into the hills you roam,
you will still come across the ubiquitous sheep.
This one was fascinated by the sight of
me battling with a new tripod.

**Afon Nant y Maen
on the Abergwesyn to
Tregaron Mountain road**
*One of so many streams that
meander down to the huge
reservoir of Llyn Brianne.*

Old barn window at Abergwesyn
Abergwesyn is a sleepy hamlet at the confluence of the Afon Irfon and Nant y Rhiw rivers.
Hill farming is the main occupation here, as it is in much of the rest of Mid Wales.

Chapel at Abergwesyn
This poor old chapel seems all but abandoned, but was doubtless a focal point of the community years ago.

Victorian post box in barn wall, Abergwesyn

I was struck by the marked contrast between the deep red of the post box and the slatey grey walls of the barn. Quite a journey for the postman too.

Church of St Michael and All Angels, Cascob
Although almost completely rebuilt in 1895, the church still retains an air of real antiquity, with its timbered tower.

Opposite: **Community Stores and Pub at Llangunllo**
A peaceful rural village, Llangunllo has its own community shop and pub.
Nearby is Llangunllo station on the beautiful Heart of Wales railway line.

Lamb suckling at Cascob
Such a typical scene in early spring in Mid Wales.

Soar y Mynydd Chapel
This Methodist chapel, hidden away in the remote hills above Llyn Brianne, is well worth a visit.
It has its own residence attached, but there is not another house or farm to be seen.

Early morning dew on spider's web at Llyn Brianne
These are real miracles of nature, shown to best effect when marked out by tiny dew droplets.

Mountain road between Abergwesyn and Tregaron
This must surely be the loneliest telephone box in Wales. Sited on the hills between Abergwesyn and Tregaron, this rarely visited spot suddenly hints at civilisation nearby.

Opposite: **Moorland fence on the Abergwesyn to Tregaron road**
Criss crossed with sheep fencing, this lonely upland area is also a favourite location for the Forestry Commission.

Picnic spot above Llyn Brianne
This is one of a handful of picnic spots offering views down onto the enormous reservoir. I decided, however, to look the other way and photograph this pair of pines.

Frogspawn on fence post at Abergwesyn
*I was attracted by the massive cacophony of frogs in this marshy valley near Abergwesyn,
when I spotted a pile of frogspawn laid on the very top of the fence post, and rapidly drying out
in the heat of the sun. A huge effort by the frog – and all for nothing.*

Opposite: **Gate onto moorland above Llyn Brianne**
*Much of the hill country around Esgair Hir, north of Llyn Brianne, is fenced and gated to keep sheep
where they should be. Lichen growing on the gate is a good indicator of clean air.*

Post Office and Stores at Rhandirmwyn
A quiet village in the Tywi Valley north of Llandovery, and an excellent base for exploratory forays into the surrounding hills.

Valley leading to Abergwesyn
Looking west along the Gwesyn Valley to the tiny hamlet of Abergwesyn, hidden among the surrounding hills.

The Drovers' Arms, Mynydd Eppynt
It is some time since ale was supped here.
Most of Eppynt is now home to an enormous
firing range run by the Ministry of Defence.
Photographed horribly early one spring morning.

**Afon Tywi running down
past Dinas Rock**
*This classic view of the Tywi just
before it is joined by the Afon Doethie
is taken from a craggy outcrop with
an interesting drop, if you walk
too close to the edge.*

Afon Pysgotwr Fawr, east of Llanddewi Brefi
It was the rusty old barn which stood out in this greener than green landscape that caught my eye. A recurring theme of Mid Wales.

Cynghordy Viaduct
Taken below the viaduct with a long lens to bring the spans of the viaduct closer together.

Opposite: **Cynghordy Viaduct near Llandovery**
This splendid viaduct on the Heart of Wales line was illuminated
in such a way that it almost defied me not to photograph it.

Pen y garreg Reservoir in autumn
Autumn with its orange and brown tints always pulls me towards the Elan Valley – and it never disappoints.

Caban Coch Reservoir in autumn
I was particularly drawn to the little tin shack almost hidden from view in the trees by the reservoir shore.

Sheep and curious offspring at Cynghordy
I have heard it said that there are more sheep in Mid Wales than people.
But they are so integral to the area they simply cannot be ignored.

Stream tumbling down into Garreg Ddu Reservoir
Water is such an influential force in Mid Wales that it often provides good subjects for the photographer.

Opposite: **Chapel on Brechfa Pool**
Brechfa Pool, above Llyswen in the Wye Valley, is a haven for waterfowl. Last time I was here, the chapel was up for sale.

Craig Goch Dam and Control House
Craig Goch is the highest of the chain of reservoirs in the Elan Valley. Some years ago there were plans to extend the reservoir up the valley but, thankfully, this came to naught. Above here is nothing but upland wilderness.

Opposite: **Cenarth Bridge
over Afon Teifi**
*Cenarth, the home of a coracle
museum, is a popular tourist spot, but
it also offers a real flavour of rural Mid
Wales based around a busy river.*

**Garreg Ddu Dam from near Nant
Gwyllt Church**
*Most of the dam is under water,
except during drought. It is the
only one in the system with a road
running along its crest.*

Logging on The Devil's Staircase near Abergwesyn
Forestry is very big business in the hills and accounts for a considerable acreage of land.

Opposite: **Old tractor near Llanddewi'r Cwm**
This is just so typical a scene in so many of the farms of Mid Wales. The tractor may be old, but it's still in use.

Hill farm near Llanddewi'r Cwm
*This scene also typifies Mid Wales to me. The mixture of rural hill farm and a rugged backdrop of hills
serves to illustrate how beautiful scenery and a very hard lifestyle are interwoven.*

Opposite: Afon Teifi at Cenarth
The building on the far side of the falls is an old mill, which is now the home of the coracle museum.

Afon Irfon at Pwll Bo, near Abergwesyn
*It was the colour and shape of the rocks on this stretch
of the Irfon known as Pwll Bo which fascinated me.*

St Harmon Parish Church
*Not perhaps the most photogenic church in Mid Wales, but one with a strong link to the
Rev. Francis Kilvert, whose parish this was after his time at Clyro.*

Brick Cottage, Tylwch
*Tylwch is a peaceful and remote village near Llanidloes, all the more so since the closure
of the railway line that split it in two. It was not so peaceful in 1899, when a mail train
and excursion train met head-on, killing one local girl and injuring five other people.*

Afon Duhonw near Builth Wells
A tributary of the River Wye (Afon Gwy), the Duhonw flows into its bigger partner at Pont Duhonw.

Looking down on the remains of the Bryn Tail lead mines
These mine ruins, right at the foot of the Clywedog Reservoir dam, remind you that it was not always idyllic and peaceful in this rural hill country.

Hillside above Llyn Clywedog
This is really the eastern lower slope of Mynydd y Groes, a rugged hillside now tamed by grazing sheep.

Opposite: **Llyn Clywedog**
More taming here too. This time it is the damming of the Afon Clywedog to form the enormous reservoir which extends for about 6 miles. I still struggle with places like this; do they make or destroy a landscape?

Angler on Llyn Clywedog
Looking very small in a very big landscape, this angler is probably after brown or rainbow trout.

Cabbage white butterfly on buttercup
*I spotted this butterfly on the Aber Biga Nature Walk, at the top of the Clywedog Reservoir.
It finally stayed still long enough on the buttercup for me to photograph it.*

Red Hill
*Typical of the Radnorshire Hills, Red Hill seems to roll on for ever. The one solitary tree serves to break
up the scene a bit. The scene is more attractive in winter because of the rich orange colours
of the bracken. Maybe that's how Red Hill earned its name?*

Opposite: **Severn Break-its-Neck waterfall**
*This wonderfully-named waterfall is such a marked contrast to the expanse of water
which passes under the Severn Bridges, yet this is the same river in its infancy, having
risen nearby under Pumlumon Fawr. The falls are deep in the Hafren Forest.*

Beech tree on the Wye near Llyswen
Taken on a superb autumn day along the Wye Valley Walk

Opposite: **Wynford Vaughan Thomas Memorial, Bryn y Fedwen**
This memorial to one of Wales' finest broadcasters is sited superbly on the mountain road between Llanidloes and Machynlleth and the hills beyond.

Pen y garreg Reservoir and Craig Goch Dam
The blue sky and white clouds, so well reflected in the Penygarreg Reservoir, sum up a perfect autumn day.

Bridge over the Wye at Builth Wells

A bridge with some very special memories for me. This is the crossing point from Builth (Llanfair ym Muallt) into Llanelwedd, the home of the Royal Welsh Agricultural Show.

The Black Mountains from the Begwn Hills
The summits of Hay Bluff (left) and Twmpa (centre) are clearly visible in the background, from this superb viewpoint high in the Begwn Hills.

Soar y Mynydd Chapel, Llyn Brianne
This tiny chapel is so remote you wonder where the congregation would have come from.

Nant Gwyllt Falls, Elan Valley
I really love the mix of greens and browns in this picture.

95

Rhulen Church
*A very pretty church, hidden away in the Radnorshire Hills, is especially
so around March when the daffodils are in flower.*

Llyn y March, Llanbedr Hill
The feeling of remoteness here is amazing; the silence is complete in a profoundly-peaceful way.
I would love to find out what the wooden butts are for?

Henllyn Lake, Llandeilo Hill
Llandeilo Hill is the upland area overlooking the village of Aberedw. The view from here stretches across to the Black Mountains.

Pen y garreg Reservoir

The second reservoir as you progress up the Elan Valley. This was a glorious day, and it took me several hours to travel a relatively short distance – you simply can't hurry through the Elan Valley.

Nant Coll Falls on Abergwesyn Common
*Abergwesyn Common is owned by the National Trust. The gorge is full of
streams tumbling down the rugged hillside to meet the Afon Irfon.*

Craig Goch Dam
Craig Goch Dam in the Elan Valley holds back the waters of the uppermost reservoir.
Plans to extend the reservoir size seem to have gone quiet.

Dylife Gorge
This deep and spectacular gorge catches you unawares on the road between Llanidloes and Machynlleth.

Barn at Bleddfa near Knighton
Typical Radnorshire barn architecture
– a real mix of local wood and stone.

Pilleth and the Lugg Valley near Knighton
The Battle of Pilleth was fought here in 1402 between Owain Glyndwr and Edmund Mortimer, the victory being decisively Glyndwr's. Mortimer ended up swapping his allegiances – and even married Glyndwr's daughter.

St Mary's Church, Pilleth
*This whitewashed church, underneath Bryn Glas Hill, overlooks the Lugg Valley,
just as it would have overlooked the fierce battle fought here in 1471.*

Wye Valley from Twmpath Hill above Erwood
*This photograph shows the contrast between the rich agricultural meadows
alongside the river and the common grazing land just above it.*

Opposite: **Low Valley, St Harmon**
*St Harmon is a small village in the hills north east of Rhayader.
This wide marshy valley rests in between the surrounding hill country.*

The Harp Inn, Old Radnor
Old Radnor is a tiny village comprising a church, a few houses and the pub. The Harp Inn dates from the fifteenth century and stands near the Wales-England border.

Old farm shed near Walton
*I found these poor remains of an
old farm shed looking utterly sad
and neglected while I was
photographing the Four Stones.*

Four Stones, Walton
Believed to date from the early Bronze Age, these are one of only a small number of four-stone circles standing in Wales.

Radnor Forest, near Kinnerton
The sheep were blissfully unaware of the photographer and his tripod, some yards away.

**Silver birches,
Radnor Forest**
*I was just putting the
camera back in the
rucksack when I noticed
the beautiful sheen on the
bark of these silver birches.*

Llan Bwch-llyn near Painscastle
The sheltered lake of Llan Bwch-Llyn viewed from Llanbedr Hill. The Black Mountains can just be seen in the distance.

Hedge laying above Painscastle
Each county seems to have its own unique way of laying hedges.
This example was above Painscastle, in Radnorshire.

Twm Tobacco's Grave on Llandeilo Hill
*Twm's lonely grave overlooking the Edw Valley. He is believed to have been a packman
travelling with his wares including, of course, tobacco, to sell to local people.*

Summer meadow at Llanstephan, near Llyswen
The summer was at its height, as were many of the meadow flowers, as I walked along the Wye Valley.

Field off the Glasbury to Llyswen road
Agriculture thrives here, as the road follows the fertile Wye Valley from Hay on Wye to Builth Wells.

Llanstephan Suspension Bridge, near Llyswen
Just peeping out of the trees, this wonderful suspension bridge, built in 1922, is just about wide enough for a car.

Painscastle

Painscastle is a sleepy village once guarded by a large castle, of which little now remains.

Church of St Michael, Clyro
This is the parish church where the Rev. Francis Kilvert was curate around 1865, when he started his diaries which have now become so well known. The tower was built after Kilvert's time.

Cottages in Clyro
These wonderfully-preserved cottages are at the east end of Clyro church, and almost certainly look today as they would have done in Kilvert's time.

Afon Edw at Aberedw
The River Edw as it passes behind the church in the village of Aberedw.

Llyn Teifi, Teifi Pools
The Teifi Pools are the source of Afon Teifi, high in the Cambrian Mountains east of Pontrhydfendigaid.
They are popular with trout fishermen and managed by Dwr Cymru (Welsh Water).

The bridge over Afon Ystwyth, Pont Rhyd y Groes
This little village stands either side of Afon Ystwyth. Its unhurried air is infectious.

Opposite: **Farm near Cwmystwyth**
*This old hill farm is typical of the dwellings in this area. Hidden in the folds of the surrounding hills
and adjacent to a huge conifer forest, it sums up rural Mid Wales perfectly to me.*

Farm barns near Nantyrhwch, north of Llyn Brianne
The rusty red of the barn really stands out against the green of the encroaching forest.

Dolgoch Youth Hostel
Accessible only by track, Dolgoch must surely be one of the most remote youth hostels in Wales.

Milestone near Beulah
A not-so-old milestone between Beulah and Abergwesyn, reminding you of where you are – and where you are going.

Maythorn tree in blossom on Abergwesyn Common
Maythorn, or hawthorn, is at its very best in the first week of June.

Red kite
*So symbolic of Mid Wales, and surely one of the UK's most successful recovery programmes,
the graceful soaring flight of the red kite never fails to impress.*

The Star Inn, Dylife
Said to be the highest pub in Wales, and certainly one of the most remote,
the Star Inn looks down on what was once a busy lead mine.

Countryside south of Machynlleth
*The valleys leading up to the hills south of Machynlleth present the eye with all shades of green
in the summer months. This shot was taken looking up the Dulas Valley.*

Farmland near Devil's Bridge
*You can walk in these green hills all day and not see a soul. Farmland and forest
combine almost seamlessly in this quiet hinterland.*

Opposite: **The infant River Wye beneath Pumlumon Fawr**
The River Wye (Afon Gwy) rises under the bald lump of a hill, often Anglicised to Plynlimmon, before its trans-Border journey to Chepstow.

The lonely bluebell
Surrounded by lush, tall grass, this lonely bluebell was buried deep in the Hafren Forest.

Cascade near Llandeilo Graban
One of many streams cascading down hillsides on their way to meet the mighty Wye.

Opposite: **Dolleycanney road junction, near Newchurch**
What a lovely old signpost – there are very few of these left.

Montgomery Castle
*Montgomery Castle, dating from the early thirteenth century,
silhouetted against a late summer evening sky.*

View east from Montgomery Castle
A peaceful summer evening, looking towards Welshpool and the border with Shropshire.

Chapel gate at Maesyronnen Chapel
*I noticed this interesting interplay between the crosses on the gate and the
Black Mountains in the background. This is truly God's country.*

Llyn Clywedog
One tiny angler dwarfed by the enormity of this remote reservoir.